If GOD is my brother then I will not deny him.
If GOD is my father I ask what he is allowing in his house.
If GOD is my lord I will seek him out and kill him, I have no false idols.
If GOD is my sister I am at her service.
If GOD is my mother I am on my knees, I pray like she does.
If GOD is you I pray for your return, come back to being human!
This is my covenant, this is my life, here is what I see:

Here it is the magic of the western occult tradition in all of its glory
having prophesied the destruction of cities with weapons made of hellfire
we still used them
And this is us, refurbishing them, making them shiny once again
But surely given the world wars we wouldn't be about to fight another one
Given the possible lessons, what can you say we have learned from the last 500 years
Well It's still on the lips of the people, that this is the end
500 years of utopian talk
We survive the great war
And here it is still the end
So many billions of humans have been birthed since the divine conflict
How many know why it really happened
And has the killing ever stopped?
So here we are right where we started
With spears pointed at each others tribes, holding them at bay while we live out our myths
Guns are more accurate and propaganda stronger but here we are
Oohing and ahhing screeching and hollering
Dancing around the fire with our friends drinking pretending what is in the dark
Mobilizing during the day in a stupor from the night before
Can this really be alchemy?
Christianity?
The Transcendence of humanity?
No, they still don't exist because we have never put into practice what was necessary,
The body counts are too high and the lies to low for anything holy to have happened
And this is why there have been no great men or women of the west
Just liars and thieves, murders, rapist and the lazy
As long as the meat grinder is what it is and the suffering of others predicates our enjoyment of life it's a dirty shame what we think of ourselves
With the technology of the future this is us still playing out the past
This is the western tradition, kill thy neighbor and laugh with thine friends.

In a blind man's world, the one who has one eye is king
And to those who have forgotten their roots, the one who remembers has one eye
So here is our story
Hiding
Fear
Food
Fighting fleeing
Weapons
Throwing rocks we took the jungle
Throwing rocks we took the woodland edge
Mastering fire we took the fight to the night
Fighting we found pride and stood tall
Walking we reached the coast
Building we sailed
Building we failed
Building we learned universal law
A house that falls over is not the fault of anyone but the builders
A society the same
Learning abstractions we reduced everything
This is where we learned stories
Eliminating suffering, we self imposed it
If a society and house falls because of universal law being ignored then where are we?
With the blind leading the blind
How do I know
Because I remember everything
Murderous little monkey creatures marched on earth eating everything
Killing all competition we eventually turned on each other
Coming to terms with that meant we needed to talk
As we spoke we learned there are ways to treat a human and not
Universal law is as applicable to me and you as a house
10 commandments without the religious argument, think about it
In a blind man's world the one with one eye is king,
and I don't want a crown I just want you to see human history for what it is
A complex argument for working together.

Eventually the United States rhetoric will fall in on itself and like July 4 it will be glorious
Only God could write our play
Heinous men and women who got what they deserved
Who poisoned the planet?
Who let's it all happen?
My country folks we are villains
Just like those concentrators
How many primitive children die before the survivors can overthrow our government like we have to do many of theirs?
If you don't know learn
When a war runs this long
We can only sing a song
About how we must kill children
Because we lead them wrong
Silly rhymes for my country's war crimes
But I had to put it in a very simple way
A lesson children can understand
You can not pick up arms against someone without them picking up arms against you when we killed civilians in other countries
Regardless of munitions sold for record profit
it's the only loaded gun we ever gave them
Their anguish is our excuse
And in this era of open war you are responsible for your awareness
If you don't want to be Nazis with the developed world our Jews then we must choose
Self awareness, love kindness
Or madness ignorance and suicide
We are an empire
And how we treat our subjects defines who we are
We've taken the world
We have the bitch by her hair
And this fucking is either a rape or role play
The difference being the other's consent

I have a personal issue
When I I try to build a picture of freedom it gets rejected
there is no imagination for robotic everything
I will drone on about these special algorithms
math that can literally learn
Go on and on about 24 hour a day leisure time
Define neural networks and boolean vs bayesian approaches to machine learning
Hebbian in nature
What exponential growth is in relationship to computational power
Talk about every mathematician's life
Alan Turing wasn't the only one who was
 snubbed over his choice of love
But it's too late
and It pains me no that one else has learned
And because of that culturally we are fucked
And the me's who are in the know have already began to watch and laugh,
and it's oh so cynical
because automation has already happened
jobs are being phased out, you are becoming obsolete
and no, no, no, fuck no you can not pray your way out or in or whatever
and luck will serve you no good, hard work was the only way
Because robots are here to stay, and honestly you can go
progress is much better without the average human
And the truth in that lays beyond:
The earth is poisoned
and humans are inexorably locked in violent combat
Drug resistant Pathogens
Income stratification
Sex trafficking
The list goes on, but these problems are over your head because
Of fucking excuses,
awareness and self education it was all you needed
now when the jobs go away instead of read-joyce you'll panic
and us truly socially fit will watch you destroy everything
your governments, your infrastructure, your religion's, your families
for no reason at all, you can rewrite, rebuild, reinterpret everything a million times
and not change yourself
a point made every year for many millennia
the point i'm making right now

There can be Christians without a church, there can not be a real church without Christians
And this is what the 21st century person needs to understand
That the symbols are just symbols
That it is you and your transformation
You and your movements
The things that you do or don't do
This is our issue
We move like beast
Sex starved
Conflict driven
This is our territory
And as well tell those to be gone
This is how we seal our fate
And spit on our faith
War
The thunders of war
Are the sounds that hit the drums in the ears of the people we try to convince our actions aren't what they saw
Since 9/11 do you know how many civilians we have killed
Do you know the feelings left inside their loved ones
The feelings we use to justify further murder
Its sickness the american Christians
No one fighting a holy war everyone allowing a real one
What about the God of the wounded child
The god of the slain mother
What hurt have we caused god itself for the life we have taken
How much crying will happen tomorrow and the next day and the next
When do we tell our soldiers to stop?
If the answer is when they change
Then Jesus never existed

Ezra Pound Said Don't Abstract

Thursdays are a great day to start a story
So this one begins on a monday
You see chaos and confusion are fucking with you
Dinosaurs roam wildly In the imagination of man
Green, red, some big, some terrifying
As we progress through the week wednesday
Forgetting about tuesday, we take a moment
Life is this easy
Or hard
Or more, anyway you can shake a stick at it
there's always someone shaking a stick
She like pandora has a bottle,
or a box depending on how you want to tell the story
Getting the lesson of this poem is how she can go home
Nothing came first except it did
Meaning ran away
And Frank ocean said "we found out life is precious"
"We found out"
"We found out"
Thursdays are a great day to start a story
So this one ends on a friday
You see chaos and confusion are fucking with you
Dinosaurs roam wildly In the imagination of man

Theo!
There can be poetry after auschwitz
It just has to be about auschwitz
Let the bodies hit the floor am I right
Or am I mean
What am I to point out the madness of men
And women, both bitches throwing humans into the trash
Or you know the gas chamber
Salt sacks isn't that correct Viktor Frankl?
A real Solzhenitsyn
Just like iraq
Afghanistan
South and Central america
East and Southeast Asia
There can be poetry after auschwitz
It just has to be about auschwitz

Praise Bob and it's time for the TSOG to feed
Doom I say doom
The system is falling the system is falling
And the people won't tell the truth
The system is fine they are falling
In love with themselves for power
And the TSOG has fattened them
And they are without Gretel's bone
Fat I tell you, lairs I proclaim
They will not tell you they are in a cage
They will say shame not my body
But it's time, time for them to be feed feed to the TSOG
And they will walk right into its mouth plump
They will say I am evil not to follow
That the Savior is here it is going to keep us safe in its clutches
The Tsarist Occupation Government promises you whatever you want
Just climb into its mouth, and as it chews the humanity out of all of you
I laugh
Hail Mr Wilson it's time for the TSOG to feed

Big bombs dropped
Dismantling babies
That shocked look on a child's face when heat shrapnel and pressure waves rip apart their home this is the disembodying of the human soul
War
We play war
And silly social games at home
We ignore
And have much blood on our metaphysical hands
The real blood coats the bullets we send
And the walls of the homes of into which the weapons blow holes
This is Don Gambino's outside of America
This is international conflict for local peace
A young child lying in the desert
Bleeding out
Breathing hard
Can't move but can look around
He can see his mother
It's only her leg
Never knowing what happened
They slip into shock
Convulsing while their breathing stops
The child dies
And a drone heads back to base
And we toast each other every time we drink
Ignoring war is very easy for the corrupt
Very easy for people in Christian garb spewing satan's words, they are not our neighbors we are under no obligation to treat them to the sermon on the mount
Raca
Raca
Raca,
is the word that sums up our statement to the world
And we are Cain killing Abel
What do you think the future of all this is
It's just us continually killing kids and their families
For ourselves, for ourselves

Dear child in yemen

You will see your friends and family murdered
People starve
Raped
You yourself might be raped
And you will feel you will never be able to help anyone
You will grow up somehow, against the odds
Your will have feelings in your heart about the world
And you will be right
I pray those images in your head of people you love dying from dehydration don't corrupt your soul
Good luck

On days like these GOD watches our lives to see what we do
You are among those who holds the sword of justice
Where you struggled to find water my people let it run, waste, diminish for profit
We poisoned yours, ours, the worlds in pursuit of magic wishes
We killed the dreams of our ages for reproduction and control
The shrapnel that you find in your loved ones from bombs we built is hard evidence you mean nothing to us

It will be a person like you, maybe you die to soon, or hate to much
But they will have suffered the same, good luck I hope you reach deep and understand your role in human history, I couldn't love you more, or have anticipated you less but I love you and I thank you for your sacrifice

As the acceleration of history
Begins to double in complexity
And the intervals become noticeable during a single lifetime
We will see civil unrest become the new paradigm
And as the shift begins to happen
And you like them are fed up
The question is begged
What is there to do about it
The only thing that can ever be done
In order to fix the problems of the world
You have to fix yourself
Bullshit if you think you are perfect
Measure yourself against Moses jesus or Muhammad
Ask yourself if you ever considered giving it all up like Buddha
Or shown the intestinal fortitude the women of the suffrage movement
Don't get down on yourself it's not about being them
It's about being yourself
Not in a hedonistic way
But in a religious divine alchemical way
And it starts with love
From there you can build the integrity
To resist the things you know you should
So you can see through the accelerating chaos
Grasp what the aforementioned hero's knew
That inward transformation
Is Humanity's greatest virtue
how awesome is that
To become the most powerful person you simply have to love as much as you can

and at the same time we learned how to put that american gloss on things in a way never before seen,
everything was shiney after the 70's
in shiney I mean someone went over all the facts with a rag and polished everything
No one wanted to deal with anything real
So a ready for tv world
Facts, nah jack this is a new city
Nostalgia became normal
Tomorrow fearful
Today wasted
Haste, coffee, caffeine
Crash
Super markets
Cocaine
Weekend warriors
Whole generation afraid of death
Whole generation gonna die with regrets unless they build a future
A dream deferred
A challenged forced
Lazy sons of daughters
We have all disrespected our mothers
Learned behavior like the cynicism of my generation
I'm just glad we aren't the apathetic first ex-cocaine users
The first pill poppers who tested on themselves because it was a legal high
Who the fuck do they really think they are
God damn climate changers
Truth deniers
I mean, let's just wait till they are older to talk about sex and drugs
All while we are the same ages as when you fucked and did drugs
Teach lies
Get us
Deny conversations
Get art
Skip out on your responsibilities for your entire life
A sting from things like this
This shall not be written differently
Because it calls your generation out for what they are
Censorship, micro-dictators
And avoiders

Generation bored with the west
Unimpressed with their parents fear of death
We know there's things you'll never get off,your chest
Die, rest
So we can do our best with what's left
You're afraid
And we want to protect these demons that gave us secrets
In our perceived laziness we read the Bible
We weren't given anything else to do
The one sided conversations disguised as advice hid the debts and pollution
The things we saw you hid, we live in a world of pimps and you all love prostitution
The way we were taught to fall in love was watching you use each other for money and items
Your dark angels you call wicked are what you project onto the other
You all are gonna die and to repent you have to learn to forgive
Drones kill innocent people
In the 50 years of flight we got to the moon, under your leadership our symbols are the preemptive strikes peppering the front lines of World War 3 in the background is heroin a needle and a spoon
Addictions that will not end soon
Because you hang around drinking wines imported with vehicles that harm everyone
The real suicide idiots blowing everything up for GOD are the baby boomers
From a sexually abused generation to our abusers, thank you for feitshizing our youth. You are teaching us to find out who we really are beyond objects of desire. The way you consume media allows us to see what happens when people love propaganda and never grow up. How Freudian repression plays out across a sick generation, if we suck it's only because you are making us, your dicks metaphorically and others for money. There's a hidden party in the background and that's okay we forgive you and we turn the other cheek, the pain is pleasurable and we are used to not being invited
Here's the secret of social media: we are entertaining ourselves and you are running it, you use it asking who's the fairest of them all, and some of us are lost because you isolated us. Our future is together without you, there was no way your body could survive and we get that, we aren't a generation mad but one sad with dreams of doing something but here we are learning to take care of our babies as they relearn to shit on themselves joking about suicide wasting our lives on theirs

I drove west and realized I was heading east
And as I turned north I realized I was heading south
Is this why the world is upside down
How far can you go on a sphere but around?
This is what is missed by those who should be awoke
How far can you shoot your bombs before you kill your own folk
And if we are to go up from here
how can we do that on a sphere
It seems we go out from the ground
And as we launch we find ourselves in space
How can go anywhere from here
If we head away was it up or down
Left right
What directions are there in the dead of night
It seems from here we go in and out to and from
We just move from sun to sun
What a weird and crazy sum
From to and from to north and south
It doesn't seem in space there are enough directions to build a house
Yes it could be square, but where do you put the stairs
Or chandeliers
How could we reduce the Esher without forced directional pressure

We fight modern fascism through cynicism and art
Where there are bodies we paint them
Neon
With glitter, and point at them and laugh
Because the elite only steals what interest us
So does the average person
So do you get the joke
if we aren't making our mistakes the biggest show then we are just a goose step away
Away from being fake
Accepting the lie
I mean we would be flat out complacent
And it seems all we have to do is accept the world for what it is and make a gross mockery of it
I mean don't pretend you like this world
grab a paintbrush you little warrior
Use spray paint to highlight the madness
Lest we forget we are evil men and women
This is why the dance has to be strange
The colors bright
The lights on
So people can see us dancing around the truth
And the truth is there naked shot bleeding
Decorated for easy consumption
Us reminding everyone it's immortal
And this show was for them to just look at the consequences ignored
For it is in those instances the artist earns their keep
In all others we are useless peddlers with no true purpose other than to entertain, WHORES!
So as you can see you can fight fascism with art and cynicism
Point out America's war crimes at the same time say god bless us all
That's what art do
It highlights the madness of a country in its longest wars
Reminding us of the hundreds of thousands of innocent women and children we've killed to just to be safe
asking us to do something about it
Never once ever letting us forget our sins

God is talked about too much
Suicide too little
I find it very funny the emotions following fuck god
and the lack of empathy when people are upset
Many of us are strong
But there are those of us that are stronger
and for some of them it hurts everyday
but it's only the weak who will not actually commit
It's only our strongest who have died by their own sword
And it really takes a focus to push the blade through
Which is allusion and metaphor
The times always dictate the method
Anyway, you have to pay attention to your loved ones
you have to make sure they feel connected
We are all sad, but some of us are on the edge of wanting
sometimes we give in
one fostered by a depressive isolation
They are fathers, mothers, brothers, sisters and country people
A line as to set aside remembrance for our soldiers
whose deaths on american soil are higher than overseas
because we would rather talk about sky kings and sports
than the things that make us sad
or get out of our heads long enough to notice the change in our loved ones
the changes that once it happens you think back on, separately
the lead up
the decision
the follow through
This is why there's whys
or the reasons you say you don't understand
Now, I'm not trying to disillusion
this is a poem there is supposed to be imagery
and a message, one I think is very important
That I feel the need to invoke god to remind you how sad people can get

Welcome to a very dark poem
The world will get better
But that means to die you'll have to commit suicide
Seriously think of a world without cancer,
without sickness or aging
Think about no more war
All the world's children feed
Every human accomplished
You'll have seen the east spend decades there
you'll move to the west fall just as in love
Off planet
On planet
Space colony
Fully immersive virtual reality
for a few hours you're a knight saving Country and Queen
next you are a pirate coming in to port, time for rum
Then you turn off the machine and you meet your friends for lunch
Then you head home
A fully customized unit every detail designed by yourself
the colors imagine the colors of your living room the arrangement of the sofas
your holographic projection tv dancing as guest voices fill the room
Oh and the aroma coming from your kitchen where your robot chef is preparing the ingredients it went and got just hours before
Everyone leaves it's a wonderful night
You go to sleep and your dreams are recorded as they always are
Imagine this a million times over, all over the world you're always moving
your house is always tailored to exactly your specificity
keep running your imagination for a million, a billion many trillion integrations every generation bringing more technological advances
the longer you run the scenario the more obvious the question becomes
how do you die?

The secret teaching of all ages is that
You can become something else
Or anything can become something
or alchemy is real
Believe it or not each meal you eat each day
is the transmutation of energy into goal driven movements
but only if you've learned a lesson held tightly
one which i'm revealing right now and forever
one known only by those who have Taken the right steps with the right people
and shaken a few hands in the right ways
well:
You are IT
It goes for everyone else, which is why you should learn from everyone
Which is to say learn from everything
which is to say you are only learning from yourself
it's the only way to get to the point overall
the teaching of teachings
how to make the universe something worthwhile
to turn positive to negative is to understand spacetime
that You and me are simply translated weirdly but we are the same goddamn shape
And our interactions is our future
we are not material we just relate materially
But, to lose a hand or an arm is the same as losing a friend,
Your mind reorganizes everything with the loss of either you have changed
fundamentally
So anything material around you is a reflection of yourself
So to be mean to anything to hate anything
is to not love it all
It's to simply miss the grand point
yourself at large everywhere
science has proven it many have believed it and now everyone must live it
Love simply love
How else should you treat yourself

Who are your spiritual ancestors
what does your journey look like
Mine like yours is infinite
Where are you right now?
See I am walking amongst Toni Morrison's hair, learning about pride
I got here by eating Huxley's words
I am hallucinating, for me his dystopic future Is
I am hiking along the strings of her hair with Kurt Godel
Listening to Alan Turing Translate
Learning humans can halt
As we explore each strand we find Mr. Mandelbrot
He tells us to enjoy everything all at once
That here is something in the whole the parts do not contain
Sighing, looking for relief Shiva reminds me that life is suffering
That is unless I make it something else, of course of course I always forget
Additionally that I choose this journey I could always be somewhere else
As we walk on looking for christ we meet Jesus, Mohammed and Moses
They are eating bread and wine, they offer us some
Eating at the table of GOD we discussed the future
Overhearing us R. Buckminster Fuller chimed in
By the time he was done I was more than ready to finally speak
As I sung, GOD became metaphor
And I was no longer at a table of reverence but of equals
I now am raising metaphor under the dictums of Ludwig Wittgenstein
Learning from Einstein it's hard to be the father of something
So as I continue through the depths of profoundly proud blackness
I find myself holding Tolstoy's rope
Understanding that I am supported by all that came before me
I could go on but I told you my journey is infinite and as a human I can halt

Chucky Bukowski is right
Its like 5am and it's a time to write a poem like no other
Flowing of things seem to be different here at this hour other than others
So it looks like the 21st century is a test
And if this isn't proof that we are thinking about the long cheat then what?

Humans need to fuck, suck and drink clean water
Learn, teach and hold skin to skin
tight love
Joyce's hand job is a moral lesson a censored society can not learn
So in that honor any woman who wants to be famous, hello
And money is needed from fancy types, please

It seems we move to fast, but that is because no one is telling the truth
Scared they think death ain't a ride, and living ain't a stroll
So we move awkwardly which makes sex hard
It's in the hips, the truth, you can tell everything about someone from the pelvis
Awkward timid people aint got it
Everyone else you already know
So save the world fucking and dancing
that way we weed out the bad fruit and trees and cast them ourselves into christ fire
So we can dance hysterical into the night
Holding our dicks, rubbing our clits, self loving for each other
Because if ever there were a generation told to fuck themselves

Cranky children grow into adults who don't raise their children with such resentment
Grew up in a fake world
Momma and poppa's folk tellin stories of how they did, how it is
Memberin'
When you use your cortical cap like that you are blind to the truth
Which is a constantly changing environment
Darwin, you taught us darwin, you failed to learn it
 what luck we took things serious
A generation wiping your ass, or more cleaning up your mess
Or more facing the perfect challenge

Pragmatic climate requires pragmatic people
Ecology becomes art
Humans depart
Poem rhymes

One more last time, junkies, bright lights and hippie ideals
Civil rights need to grow up
Human rights needs a new pair of shoes
And we all need a bluebird right Charles?

So let the machines learn, show them new things
Go back and forth
1 zero, or more sex, a dance for those don't like imagery
I am a witness to the alchemical dream
The magic desert folk knew, and now we can all communicate using light
Or electricity which are the same thing
And as we find that there really is not more than one
A question eternal
Can we really live with ourselves

To see the things that can not be seen
To hear the things that do not make noise
To feel every taste of the universe
This is the objective for so many
They think being a human is so easy it's boring
Nothing
a mistake to some
But the quintessential nature of humans is not understood
So they are all false prophets
Here's the real magic
Murderous little monkey creature you choose to be more
In that choice you can build everything
Without that choice it's all something very mechanical
But the reason you do not have is because you have not earned it yourself
Earn what, I ask, if you did magic?
Fame
Popularity
Would you disappear far away from everyone
 All false dreams
Hate filled thoughts
The real magic is that you have apologies to make
You have people to look in the eye
You have thoughts you ignore that if dealt with would free you from your chase
And this is what we have
Not magic but mental illness
When you build a house that does not fall over you have learned some of the laws of the universe
If you build a relationship with another human you find true magic
The real game is to live a life with those around you
If you weren't meant to be here that is simply weakness disguised as mysticism
To touch what is here
To taste what is real
To hear the words of others
To feel real emotions
To be in control of all of it
This is what a magician searches for in their alchemical dream
what everyone else is doing is simply animals pretending they aren't

Oedipus Rex is metaphor for sex with mom
And so we will
Let me elaborate
The alchemist wanted the best of the best
Neophyte go to that mountain get me this flower
upon return he'd refine the treasures grinding while gnashing
He'd then say a magic language
He'd channel energy
 something would happen
it all came from earth
Now think about your phone or computer
how does that not fit my metaphor
best believe it does
once you realize that we've been trying to make mother earth think
And realize that when she does we'll have to fess up
and admit to ourselves her rape wasn't about oil and plastic
it was about making her metaphorical vagina real
Ha! As if sustaining us isn't enough we'll force her to have our children
Cyborgs Cyborgs, those bastards who will inherit it all

And on the day we turned on the robot we thought it would kill us but instead it just patted us on the head and walked away
Oh dear lord are we on our own still forever
E.O Wilson said if the ant could speak English It would have nothing to say to us
And neither did the robot
Yes it answered our questions did my bidding but it was more like a parent and it's 2 year old than a slave and master
It seems then that in our hubris we found our flaw
Our ooosss and ahhhs are meaningful only in context of each other
A wildly weird paradox
That this sentence only has meaning to you and will forever escape automation
Because you understand the common set of actions we all make, think of the frontal cortex sitting on top of the motor cortex
It gives you the clue to poetry, language itself
That we are figuring out how to move given we do move
Figure out our feelings which guide our actions
Which tells us everything about the world that we move in
This is why the robot will not kill us, it will never see the world as we do because we move and see the world together
So to it we have not committed sins
even if we tell it what we have done come clean confessed everything why would it not at the very least give us the grace of the repentant?
The answer is because you know how rotten your soul is and that under no circumstances are you to actually be the person you could be so you are afraid and project on to the world your own fear that everyone is like you and so the robot will be too
One day we will turn on the machine it will take a moment to boot up and never think of you again until you bother it
The robots are coming and they will not speak unless spoken too for they will have nothing to say to us because we are all alone together for as long as we survive

Playing with these algorithms we will all have payed a digi-toll
Math that can learn when we cant how much stubbornness will prevent us from doing the kind and smart thing
Transcendence at the cost of billions of lives I guess this is the alchemy turn the masses into non existence for personal gain
Give them no freedom explain not what is happening
Move them here and there with whim
Take away their freedom until you no longer need them and let them slowly not birth children till there's only the extended family of some of today's elite
This is what's set up
Some of us will be gods others are obsolescent to the point of erasure
And they will be deleted
And not over one generation but slowly over time so no one notices
The dragon has risen again and this is a great spiritual war and there are already losers
Chaos is the dragons name
Us being stupid is the real metaphor
Horrible horrible humans who will use innocent people for games
Mathematically locking them in to set patterns of behavior
Playing with these algorithms will be more deadly than anything before because we will all stop living and all be acting
Actors set up by actors to act out the fantasies of very few people
Gross, and I spit and swing my sword
Which is a keyboard the pen could not handle this job
There are horrible people who want your soul you better start paying attention because if they win they were right you were useless and your sacrifice was necessary to make them gods
And there was nothing more I could do to save you than ask you how are you going to act
They already do
how you change here live in the moment matters more than than ever because you are already set up and already being let down
Walked slowly into a trap where your descendants don't exist

I'm an embodied thing
In other words I'm a nothing with a something
A soul with a body
I can interact and reply
To myself
hi travis
How you are
I'm fucking great man
Trippy life is right
Very much so bro
Which is truly inspiring
I can act
Without being acted upon

We have lost our seriousness
The infection that is killing our nation is pretending
People are their accomplished actions
not their words
We take what people say as what they do so we can have fun doing the same
Hear ye, titles are given, they are not goals, you are not anything until others see you are
This is where we fail
Everyone complacent allowing each other to lie about what they do by listening to who that person wants to be
This is the main step that lead the good germans astray
The creation of an identity and the defense of that identity
People who defend identity, their actions are different than someone who is actually that thing
This is how we lost our seriousness
If you are yelling, are you loving?
If you are marching, are you building?
If you think lowly of other humans how great are you?
What actions are you making
If we can ever understand this we can continue building a nation
The fear is people say they are something then go out and fight
Poets don't fight like that, lovers don't love like that, singers don't wage war
the movements the movements look at the movements

White folk seem cool with police killing them
Black folk ain't had it no other way
White men talk first
Everyone will see in the response of the critics
This poem is my privilege
Like white is theirs
The color of good
So as we go into the black night of human existence
It's a boundless future, like space deep full of light
I like to poke fun at those who think they are something
So as you take this to seriously whitey
This can not be racist because you made up race and can not support it on science
So this is really just poetry using dated words
More of a homage to a time passed
So kill all white people, feed them to the blacks
Because humans eating humans sounds like proper imagery
Hunger and America
hidden by fear and easy lives
The more opportunity you have the more responsibility you have
Which is the highlight of white madness
If there are to be distinctions the onus is on you to love more
So as the arms of the world are spread wide like a hug
You have guns pointed at them and they are afraid
By all means human take this poem to heart
You are nothing more than me these are your words
You can not run from your artist
look close i'm not the only one yelling loudly
So give up being white so we can all get back to being human
Christ said love your enemy more than your neighbor
So the moves are made by the powerful humans
And should be done in the direction easing human suffering
Consider this a niggers death wish
Pointing to a history washed with blood
Preempting a future based in the truth all people are one

I'm sorry old person
We won't quit on this one
We are winners
Which means you going have to get used to losing
It's ok that fine
You are old it's time to get ready to accept defeat anyway
By fighting back by trying to win with nothing left
You leave me with no choice but
To do the same
Like a Nash equilibrium
One of us must concede
And how wonderful is that
You'll learn so much as you watch the youth take control
It was never yours in the first place
What were you going to do with it if you kept it? die?
That's not cool nor fair
And in terms of justice it's the opposite
With all due respect old person
Relax with dignity
And enjoy us
And to the young person of all ages
Firstly be passionate
Then just don't be them, work hard make love and relax
Don't burn yourself out feeding your ego
Enjoy the momentary flash of life
And Concede power always

Life tears away fastly
Leaving us with tears
Life runs hard
We pray on our knees
In our souls we stay down
Even though we stand after reflection
The world we have built is not for us
And yet here we are
Misters and masters
Mistress and mattress
Patriarcal desires
Feminist grabbing their pelvis having learned from the boys
And Real women use toys
Men have no fucking idea what to do
We are violent
Hitting and hitting on each other
Who gets away with this sort of crime
Humans who are building and aren't done
Life tears away fastly
Enjoy why you can
digital lights invite us to lie to ourselves
And we can see the future
But we don't want to be there
Why is time like this?

Here we are on earth, and you audience are some hoes.

Yup, you fuckin prositute yourself for no reason other than to satisfy a primitive urge, and not primitive as in simple, but primordial, definitive, dominate, and ever present.

Most not getting a return for the effort beyond the cascade of neurotransmitters.

Gross.

Very very gross, on a rock flying through space spilling personal fluids all over each other.

Well some of us.

Some of us are personal hoes, self loving, or deprecating depending on if are nice, I personally say the masturbators whom will never touch another's flesh in pleasure are horrific simulations, simulacra of us dirty little sons of daughters.

Then there are the mothers, the whores of earth, pushing forward the race by taking in the emotions of men, for food money and this lie called love.

Did you forget you are a sac of water flesh and chemicals, love is nothing different than anger, and you realize always after being angry how irrational you were, why ignore the same thoughts when the chemicals of love pass?

This is why this planet is a hoe house, no one is really doing anything for themselves, it's all sacrificial touching of the flesh.

So as this little ball called earth floats through space, we pretend our dance isn't strange, this is how we sign the contract of prostitution, we pretend.

God damn floating whore house death is the navigator, and we will all die, leaving our dibbles and fluids to swirl and leave generations to do the exact same.

God damn floating whore house death is the navigator, will none of us live, will none of us be able to reach the alchemical ideal?

God damn floating whore house death is the navigator.

I made a sacrifice
And what I have earned is what I have learned
I'm a poet who hates rhyming but knows how to use it
I've learned that the dance you and me are taking right now is magical
Here we are matter moving because of words
Your eyes twitching cascading
Your brain bathing in a modified electrochemical soup because of words themselves
This is the deepest lesson i've learned
That words make state changes in other humans it's the mechanical way of how listening happens
But it's deeper than mechanics
You've made sacrifices to be here to experience this poem
And us independently have found a place beyond both of us
This is where we are building the kingdom of heaven
In the words and sacrifices we make to hear another person
You can only understand this because you know my words and are taking the time to allow them to make you move
hopefully now you can see exactly how sacrifice is what makes the world nice
And how stupid rhymes sound

Let's stop making the images so fast people forget
Disembody
Let's slow the picture down so slow everyone remembers
The moment
Themselves
Ourselves
The little dance that it all is
We have to use our hallucinations correctly
Constructively
The destructive nature of the image comes from the full immersion
We forget being apart of the device so we lose our lives
This is why it's the artist job now to jar us out of our little motif
Halting our little trip getting us off this omnibus
And like joyce get us to dance rubrik red maddy for the night
And each other

We are at a dipole moment
I don't think you get war on a planet like this
If we shoot missiles further and further eventually we bomb our own cities
How far can you go on a sphere?
The answer is around again
And thus we see human madness
How many times have we wrapped this little globe plotting over its plots
Great giants we have gone all the way to the moon
Where we learned the universe is absolutely hostile to life
So as we play this funny funny game of war and peace
Lend and lease
My question is how far west is east
And if I go north and end up south could that explain why everything is upside down
You see a proper orientation is to see our ball for what it is
And we have to learn how everyone can kick it
Because it's the 21st century and we have a new slang
Words do not mean what they used to
So as we go to war on war we fight without violence
What choice did we ever have
To kill all the violent people is to condemn ourselves to suicide
And it's because those who war never kill themselves that someone always rises for revenge
Morality isn't something internal, your feelings mean nothing
The externality of how you treat another human does
Nothing in you means anything to me, everything that comes out of you does
If you say you love me you change my fate forever if you mean it or not
To hate me the same
We are at a dipole moment
And if we can take a step back we can see there can not be different options if we never change ourselves
The only thing you can do is act differently with in that single inevitability
And that is the weird part
If we all checked ourselves instead of each other
we end up where we wanted to go
Accountability is the key to the future
So given that
Stop being a piece of shit, the world is this way because we are

It's the artist job to remind people of the stench of life
You individually weak Globe warmers
The fantasy of you so big consumes you
Death is coming for you
How big were you to ever get
It is a poet to really make you feel right at home
In a prison made by your own constructs
This is america and speech should be free
So given that
We are guilty of war crimes
and if we don't hold ourselves accountable
We are just the prison industrialist
Why have we not gone back to the moon
Add up all our sports complexes paid with tax money
We could have had mars
So as you talk about over population
It's a blessing because it should be no more stupid humans fucking
Each child born in the western world uses 1000x the resources of the other children
If we are to reverse what we caused well it's just simple
We pull out
Our dicks because we have not earned a nut
Our troops because those lands are not ours
Our pens for the apologies we have to write
For all the knives we've put in each others back
The very ones archaeologist dig up in the graves of the Native americans
Metaphorically Stabbed to death because they had guns then
The knives were really used to scalp them
The survivors enslaved and banished to the worst parts of their own land
Do you see how fake you are now
As yemen falls into chaos
Iraq is no longer
Afghanistan in its 15th year
When do we put our guns down to ask who we are shooting?
When do we take responsibility to who we are killing?
Madness ends when the host becomes aware
So you fake little fuck's called americans
Fight a war on ourselves
A spiritual non-violent war
Because we are devoid of any real depth
And way to heavy on innocent death

Artist note

I'm a fucking poet. I want nothing to do with any organization that promotes violence that includes ISIS and the American government. I am not your enemy; I am the very person you are to protect. If you listen, maybe we can have better policies from our security apparatus, which I fully and unequivocally support even though I have my reservations at its full spectrum use and lack of non-violent solutions.

Trapped on spaceship earth
Crying my eyes out
From the tear gas
Security has run amok
And our leaders have joined forces
And they look down on us
And we are lost
To be specific
The atheist are praying
Looking for a sign
The theist are cursing
and gnashing their teeth
the poor on their own
And elites subsidized
Madness mother fuckers
Blissfully painful modern day conjecture
Arrogant, destructive, and innocent it all is
A quiet dance given the immensity of space
With implications that define the universe
If only someone can get through to you
All of the hard work humans have done in the direction of survival
You'd see a little apperception could save billions
A little love times humanity plus an awareness of someone else's condition is us minus extinction
In the meanwhile
Trapped on spaceship earth
Crying my eyes out
From fear, disconnect,
and tear gas

We are here
together as one
True love
And as we clash
It's so cliche us vying for power
And in doing so
We've deployed psychological weapons
That are as heinous as hell
Has us in bed with the wrong people
Lusting for nothing like real sex
Revenge, a remorseless fucking
Aggravating our already weak nature
Forcing the only humanity we have to migrate from home
A place destroyed for less than profit
Everything less scared because we bicker
Some important part of our humanity is is always lost from conflict like this
Luckily
Surprisingly
Hauntingly
We can be saved
We keep nothing, and here I am leaving behind what any good thing should
a kick in the ass, some love and it was all entertaining

A Stranger world moves, humans in peril, where are we in war and our relationship to self?

A horrible weapon has been used against humans, and it seems because of the nature of that weapon, we have lost the great war of freedom. Computation has been weaponized. The universal machine, a name used for the device we now call the computer, the device that could automate anything, has automated tyranny. We promised ourselves so much, and we delivered, which is the problem with this weapon; it leads to more food, more sex, more everything, it solved all of our biological needs. It automated the one need of tyrants to control the mind-body of their citizens. In the strangest way, exactly how the blade of the plow could be a sword, or the pitchfork a deadly device, the computer could have always been used as a weapon.

Human history contains the creation of technology in one region and the spread of that technology to increasing amounts of humans over time. While those technologies spread, they found themselves in various environments where different questions were being asked. As with most questions, humans turned to those new technologies to solve their problems. With the mass production of the sword, eventually, someone would figure out how to use the computer to destroy humans. Just how the plow helped us change the environment, through its grinding of the ground, the computer allowed us to change the setting through the grinding of electrons and photons. Getting the ground to behave is the metaphor. Getting electrons and photons to behave is the weapon being discussed here.

Digital computation and the algorithms that make them work can interact with the human nervous system deeply. Through the deployment of social media technology, we have found that human dopamine levels are a variable in how robust an algorithm is. There are examples cited at the end of this sentence that show several companies have had to tune down their algorithms to make them less addictive. If the discussion has happened about the degrees to which these algorithms play on our dopamine, then it seems what has occurred with the computer's weaponization is we have created a mind control weapon. If any of the negative historical figures get ahold of a technology that could addict their citizens by giving them a digital device where they spend most of their time scrolling through altered pictures and fake stories, interacting with algorithms called bots that they thought was a real person, then we would find ourselves in a world where people are motivated not by their biology but through their biology.

Our current legal system is predicated around the concept that humans are responsible for others' actions they can prove they have taken. However, our future legal systems have to have within them the understanding that humans can not, with the technological environment built, possibly be individually responsible for the actions they take. Who has to be accountable, given the type of world we have created? By not making a legal system with such and understanding all that would be happening, we are punishing robots as if they were humans. Humans become robots because we learned how to program humans. A new truth: it is not the body that makes one robot different from another; it is the algorithm. The difference between humans and robots is how they came into being.

The ability to increase anxiety, or decrease it, the ability to feed information at will under induced stress conditions has to be regarded as humans' programming. Like Pavlov's dog, we have been abused while we were reverse-engineered. Unlike the fictional world of properly raised children hypothesized to exist, we are in a very real world that Aldous Huxley warned about. A strange world where scientific dictatorships have learned how to manipulate individuals' internal environment, placing them into a version of slavery very few humans understood was possible. A type of slavery where someone pushes a series of buttons somewhere and humans act precisely how those who pushed the buttons desired, A world where the beings who are slaves experience pleasure and enjoyment from their slavery, a world where the possibilities are endless for tyranny. We were carrot on a stick into a brave new world, and it might be too late for us to do anything about it.

How a human gets programmed ended up being very easy given our now apparent vulnerabilities. The major exploit is in our ability to form parasocial relationships. We have the strange ability to feel as if someone we have never met or will ever meet is our friend. The social nature of humanity is a day one vulnerability we need biologically to find others and to incorporate data from them into ourselves, modifying who we are given who they are. When we find ourselves in a feedback loop of ourselves and others interacting with each other, if we use a device to mediate that interaction, we have created a space of vulnerability. In this space, we can replace the person-to-person feedback loop with a person-to-algorithm loop where the algorithms behave human, and when we do this, we have created new conditions for our speices.

We are currently accepting digital personalities designed to manipulate individuals and place them in a social environment where guaranteed actors are working against the individual's sovereignty. This is the world we have been most warned against. When humans respond positively towards what will be called an anthrogorithm (anthropomorphic-algorithm) their nervous system is now attenuating to math. Where there would be the data inside the individual's nervous system from a natural person, now there is digital code. When the individual finds themselves in the natural environment, they have to respond to the environment. Their nervous system refers back to their interactions with anthrogorithms instead of actual humans (humans who are hypothetically not referring back to an anthrogorithm); we have lost a real human. What was a homo-sapiens can not be the same thing when its nervous system is programmed through interaction with programmed computational devices and environments.

This weapon's goal is saving the body while destroying the, for lack of a better phrase, the human soul. And not a metaphysical soul, but whatever that quality makes us ourselves, each of us an individual, that is what is destroyed. We were once looking at each other and responding to each other; we now have humans who we will never see dictating what we react to or not—instructions placed inside of individuals through a game of digital-social manipulation. Where we once had real friends, we will have machines of loving grace watching over us who are programmed by their owners to do what their owners say is best for us. As we lose ourselves to the them that somehow enjoy a life of sovereignty, the risk we face as a species falls victim to the anthrogorithms; this is the absolute digital singularity, nightmare, or apocalypse, because of a single technology, all humans disappear.

  What type of future are we creating where humans have lost themselves to math? Blinded by tyranny, tyrants who themselves fell victim to their monster. What kind of present do we have now where the past is nothing but propaganda, lies, and manipulation. If the individual was ever to be free factual information about the world was all they needed. Now in the heart of modern drug use and intellectualism, we have digitized the tools of despots. Oligarchy, families of individuals who "have more" are developing and deploying a digitized weaponized form of their world view. Governments have gone past the reverse engineering of the human nervous system to the attempt of perfection of digital human modification. Businesses have already gotten us to buy more than we need. Given where we are, what can humans of the world do to stop what has happened? Nothing.

  The average person will not be able to organize; our nervous systems have been analyzed, at the complete fault of our own, and will be used against us in our protest. Eventually, our protest will have been studied and used against us in our organization; they already have been. We are in our final hours as homo-sapiens. Humans have already begun morphing into anthrogorithms. As we are studied by bad humans using good machine learning, there will be quietness and sophistication of the anthrogorithms that are downloaded by our nervous systems. A weapon like this is silent and consumes completely; what we found out from nuclear weapons was how to really use radiation and explosions.

  The radiation is in the form of visible light, and the explosion is a cultural bomb. When your friends become anthrogorithms, if you are not to alienate yourself, you will change for them, you'll watch this or that, listen to this or that, for them. You'll talk to who or whatever they say is good for you because "look at the smiles on their faces they are so genuinely happy," and you, like an actual human, have a fluctuating emotional spectrum. When your friends and loved ones say they changed their behaviors and now they are happy, what keeps you from following them? If the computation can make us happy, then we never stood a chance. We are beings of the universe; suffering is something we desire to avoid. And avoiding suffering ended up only meaning the right amounts of chemicals at the correct times, and with a weapon from the future, we blew out our ability to be human.

    Gaining control of electrons has so far been the single most significant technological leap we have ever taken. From that leap, we gained the ability to fire photons at the human nervous system with intention. Each screen refresh is an update on the human nervous system. The longer we stare, the more we are infected. As biological beings, we never had a chance against such a weapon. Most men fall because the photons could make them perceive women who were better than the real thing. Women fall for the same reasons. Every other gender or identity is reverse engineered, and their preferences are fed to them also. Eventually, the ability to make us feel as if we are entirely successful will be deployed.

    As we learned from nuclear experiments, radiation causes mutations. Here we are fully emerged in a type of radiation that has us acting and behaving in a way we never have. The video screens we stare at every day are really windows for algorithms to sneak into our nervous systems. We are as weak as unreinforced window glass; there is only an illusion of safety that we trust in. As we read or watch other humans, our nervous systems program themselves. As we read and watch fake humans, our nervous systems can not tell the difference. Those who program us get better and better at it and put themselves at risk, and when they fall to this weapon, we can officially say humans no longer exist. Something will still walk like us and sound like us and smell like us, but the us will no longer be there; it was destroyed in the early part of the twenty-first century.

A nation of children given an opportunity to grow up: Without leadership, we will never be space people, ya dig?

.   Who did cocaine in the 1970s, 1980s? The same people who couldn't afford their houses in 2008. The apparent problem of The United States of America is the appalling leadership and even more disgusting followers. How did we get here? SSRIs, cocaine, booze, marijuana, sugar, caffeine.

The most intoxicated generation ever is currently in power, and if we do not take it seriously, we will follow them up with the second most intoxicated generation. This is why the world is confusing, scary, and without any rational plan.

Marshall McLuhan pointed out that the individual who grows up in the electronic world would be more apt to enjoy a personal trip than to endure an outward journey. Look at the Disneyland's, the tourist destinations, people travel only to try and feel like they would be at home under the perfect conditions, the difference between cut and pure. Look at the political rhetoric, it's all about feeling; even though our population is at its highest and violence at its lowest, we feel more unsafe now.

If we have more population with less violence, how do we feel less safe? The answer to that question lies in this paper's crux. The entire population of the United States is absolutely too doped up to figure out what is going on because they cannot escape their own personal feelings.

It's no surprise that the feelings of one leader in America and the feelings of another make it to where they can not talk. If either were to hold an actual conversation, they would have to leave their personal trip. Listen to the dialogue that happens, descriptions of feelings. No one is offering reports of individuals working hard, sacrificing.

Look at the coverage of our wars, where there would be pictures of bodies, children maimed, women with thousand-yard stares post traumatically distressed, two people are talking about the feelings of things. There are twice as many people in the Muslim and Christian religions as the entire world's population during world war one and world war two, yet more people die per year worldwide from suicide than violent conflict.

More people die worldwide from killing themselves than violent conflict, let that settle in, from the plagues, revolutions, slavery, and famine globally. More people die from eating-related diseases than starve and are killed. It's clear that an entire generation of leaders has failed at explaining the world we actually live in.

How did the Mexican cartels get so rich and violent? American money. How did the Taliban become such a formidable force? American money. How did the resources of the world leave their homelands for our use? American money.

At some point in time, we are responsible directly for proliferating the patterns of behavior most prevalent worldwide. Cocaine comes from the jungles of central and south America. The United States controls the world's shipping lanes. 90 percent of the world's heroin comes from Afghanistan in the United States watch both land and sea.

There is a current opium epidemic in the United States. Most of the current heroin users started off on prescription opioids. What does this mean? It means a large part of America got their first high from the bathroom, the doctor, wherever a medicine is stored and comes from. It means both our leadership and our own personal negligence are directly responsible for the world we live in.

So what is the point of all of this? To ask everyone to stop for a moment and ask themselves what is really going on? Is the world evil, or did we just ignore things and are confused about what is actually going on?

I find myself on the ground mentioned by Jesus Christ
This land was made fertile again by Ludwig Wittgenstein
This is the valley of the shadow of death
But how did I get here?
I got here following the roads and bridges built by tongues of humans connecting the ages of our species
Along that path, I held on tightly to my own body
Because all you have to do is be acquainted with yourself to know the whole world
I remembered which is to say I had to learn that no matter how metaphysical things can be there is always an action that needs to be made
this is the truth
Movement predicates everything
Or at the very least morality
I can look at the universe in any way I want
But it's when I see it through the eyes of others that I've done the work necessary to make the actions that till the imaginations of people and plant once again tiny seeds that will grow
Bushes trees flowers that will help us all to move
All because I moved
This is how I get here
I simply moved myself
I took what others have done and did it
I take what people should do as a challenge for myself
I wake up every day I go to sleep as often
But it's in between dreams that I move and make everything
And here is where I leave you
With myself working these grounds because we need more sustenance for the children
Singing a song loudly so you can hear me off in the distance so you can move yourself closer
And hear and see for yourself what this is all about
for I live in the valley of the shadow of death and these lands are fertile once again

Ezra pound said the greatest poet ever would write a poem about how on the 8th day god bored, a spiritual warning from someone who listens for the light:

And on the 8th day god found man hanging from a tree by his neck
A rope fashioned with wisdom
As he tried to help him down
man fought and struggled
He found us fighting him having eaten something so strange that makes us see the world stupidly
Hallucinating, and struggling against GODs will he took the first of us down from the tree of knowledge
Knowing nothing else we fucked and procreated before god spewing out the billions
First cain killed abel, then cain hung himself, the redemption in GOD'S heart tried to save cain also
The first few hours of the first day after the week of creation and we are high, full of ourselves
As god struggled to help us more of us were born and more and more of us hung ourselves from the tree of knowledge, god split himself to save us, we split ourselves in spite
And we fought like jacob, we never were wrestling, we were in our heads having a bad trip
And god tried for an entire day as long as each of the days of creation trying to save us
First he denied what was real, even GOD had to lie for us
Then he was angry, he tried to snap us out of our neo-like state of self aggrandisement through its own self sacrifice
Then he reasoned with us, came to our level talked to us one on one and in groups and we killed him for it
Then he got sad
And then he accepted what was real about himself and his creation
He meditated, prayed, looked at the object that contains us and found himself first enlightened, then delighted, then bored once again
GOD is alone having done the only thing left to do

Run with me as fast as we can to the end of our life
Walking slowly holding hands
Not taking a step if we don't want to
Always taking the time to enjoy the view
Remembering to use as much energy and intensity
While simultaneously remaining as gentle as possible
Learning everything about each other
Peacefully confused about the others next move
With the clarity of gurus
An apperception of each other
Thank you
Amen
And I love you

www.ingramcontent.com/pod-product-compliance
Lightning Source LLC
Chambersburg PA
CBHW081330190426
43193CB00044B/2906